Lithuania Travel Guide

Sightseeing, Hotel, Restaurant & Shopping Highlights

Olivia Smith

Copyright © 2014, Astute Press
All Rights Reserved.

No part of this publication may be reproduced, stored in a retrieval system, or transmitted, in any form or by any means without the prior written permission of the publisher, nor be otherwise circulated in any form of binding or cover other than that in which it is published and without similar condition being imposed on the subsequent purchaser.

If there are any errors or omissions in copyright acknowledgements the publisher will be pleased to insert the appropriate acknowledgement in any subsequent printing of this publication.

Although we have taken all reasonable care in researching this book we make no warranty about the accuracy or completeness of its content and disclaim all liability arising from its use

Table of Contents

Lithuania 6
   Culture 7
   Location & Orientation 8
   Climate & When to Visit 9

Sightseeing Highlights 10
   Vilnius 10
      Republic of Užupis 11
      Museum of Genocide Victims 12
   Curonian Spit 13
   Šiauliai 14
      Šiauliai Aušros Museum 15
   Park of Europe 15
   Hill of Crosses, Jurgaičiai 17
      Franciscan Monastery 18
   Augštaitija National Park 18
      Museum of Ancient Beekeeping 19
   Panevėžys 19
      J. Masiulis Bookstore 20
      Panevėžys Local Lore Museum 21
   Kaunas 22
      Old Town 22
      Kaunas Jazz Festival 23
      Kaunas International Film Festival 23
   Klaipėda 24
      Theatre Square 24
      Castle Museum 25
      Klaipėda Picture Gallery & Sculpture Park 25
   Open Air Museum of Lithuania 26

Recommendations For The Budget Traveller 29
   Places to Stay 29
      Dalija Hotel 29
      Sandra & Co 30
      A5 Hotel 30
      Hotel Velga 31
      Hotel Alanta 31

Places to Eat 32
    Pinavija Café & Bakery 32
    Grizzly Grill 33
    Kybynlar 33
    Cukatos Bakery 34
    La Dolce Vita 34
Places to Shop 34
    Old Market in Klaipeda 35
    Linas-Medis Suvenyrai 35
    Panorama 36
    Akropolis 36
    Senamiesčio Krautuvė 37

Lithuania

The small country of Lithuania is one of the three Baltic States (with Latvia and Estonia) and is an emerging tourist destination in the era of low-cost flights in Europe. Lithuania is a great destination for a relaxing vacation and has an interesting capital city in Vilnius, beautiful rivers, lakes and forests. Natural areas occupy large parts of the country.

Lithuania is a scenic country located by the Baltic Sea. The history of Lithuania has made its inhabitants a bit reserved. It can take time to gain trust but once that's achieved Lithuanians can become good friends.

Don't miss the beautiful coastline. Rent a bike and ride the bicycle path to explore the coastline of the Baltic Sea. Rural tourism opportunities are everywhere – you can relax in a cozy countryside guesthouse or visit one of the many campsites, farmhouses and eco-tourism sites.

Lithuania is a great city break location. Many inexpensive flights arrive in Vilnius, the capital of Lithuania, with its historic sights and nightlife. In the summer season Vilnius' resplendent streets are bustling with locals and tourists enjoying the city life.

Culture

As in the other Baltic states of Latvia and Estonia, music and dance play a big role in the life of traditional Lithuanians. In the Baltic States songs were the main weapons of rebellion against the oppressive state and even today Lithuanians express their proud spirit through songs.

Since 1924 the World Lithuanian Song Festival has been held every summer. During this festival thousands of singers, standing shoulder to shoulder, unite to sing about their country, its suffering and its joy. The songs are beautiful and they are enjoyable even if you don't understand the Lithuanian language. This tradition is now shared through the Song Festival.

Lithuanians experienced many hardships during Soviet times and their traditional Sutartinės songs elevated their spirits. These polyphonic songs are not often heard outside the country. In fact in 2010 they were awarded a place on the UNESCO Representative List for the Intangible Cultural Heritage of Humanity.

Lithuanians love theatre and opera performances and the most well known theatre is the Lithuanian National Opera and Ballet Theatre, operating since 1923. Classical music fans also highly rate the Lithuanian National Philharmonic orchestra.

Lithuanians just love to discuss basketball and their team is one of the best in Europe and the world. Basketball is serious business in Lithuania!

Location & Orientation

Lithuania is the largest of the three Baltic States. It is situated in the northeastern Europe. The neighboring countries include Poland, Latvia, Belarus and Kaliningrad (a Federal "Oblast" that belongs to Russia). The Geography Institute of Paris has stated that Lithuania is located at the very midpoint of Europe, a fact that is easy to overlook. The exact centre is in the northern Lithuania about 26km away from Vilnius, close to the village of Purnuškės.

The topography of Lithuania is mainly flat, with a few hilly areas in the western and eastern parts of the country (but only 300 meters above sea level).

In common with the rest of the Baltic States, Lithuania is easy to reach by plane. There are four airports in the country - Kaunas Airport, Vilnius Airport, Siauliai International Airport and Palanga Airport. The road infrastructure in Lithuania is also good and coach or private car travel is common as well. The biggest port in Lithuania is situated in Klaipeda where international passenger ferries arrive daily.

Climate & When to Visit

The four seasons of Lithuania are very diverse, in fact you might say that there are four different Lithuania's to experience.

The most attractive season is summer with the warmest month of the year being June with average temperatures of 20°C (32°F). Maximum temperatures however can reach up to 30°C (86°F). This is the peak time for tourism in Lithuania with thousands of tourists and locals wanting to spend holiday time in the sun at the seaside resorts and in other outside locations.

Autumn and springtime in Lithuania can often be rather cold, windy and rainy; hence you should carefully check the forecasts prior choosing to go there at this time of the year.

Most often the coldest month of the year is January when the air temperature can drop to -30°C. Many are not comfortable with such cold weather, but some come then to take part in the snowsports on offer during the winter. There are places to ski, snowboard and skate – but wrap up warm!

Sightseeing Highlights

Vilnius

Vilnius Tourist Information Centers
Vilniaus g. 22
Tel: +370 5 262 9660
Didžioji g. 31
+370 5 262 6470
Geležinkelio g. 16
Tel: +370 5 269 2091
Šventaragio g. 2
Rodūnios kelias 2-1
Tel: +370 5 230 6841
www.vilnius-tourism.lv

Vilnius, the capital of Lithuania, is a city which has experienced many important events in the history of Lithuania.

The historical atmosphere can be experienced by taking a stroll on the streets of the old town.

The outskirts of Vilnius are rather dreary. Massive, grey, solid-looking mansions are a constant reminder of the oppressive ideology of various Soviet regimes – at that time any ostentation was unacceptable and everything and everyone were encouraged to look equal and similar.

On the contrary, the central area of Vilnius is green and filled with art and culture. There are significant monuments, great architecture as well as entertainment, nightlife and restaurants. In 2009 Vilnius was awarded the title of European Capital of Culture.

Gediminas Hill and Tower, Hill of Three Crosses, Vilnius University, Vilnius Cathedral and the Frank Zappa monument are just a few of the places of interest. Visit one of the tourist information centers prior to your sightseeing to pickup brochures and maps of the area. Main sites are quite close to each other, many of them are free of charge but entrance to some only costing 2LTL ($0.76) for students and children (in that case, do not forget your student ID) and 5 LTL ($1.90) for adults.

Republic of Užupis

The Republic of Užupis is probably the most extraordinary sightseeing highlight in Vilnius. It is a republic (separate territory) founded by local artists and it even has its own constitution. Sometimes it is even referred to as the fourth republic of the Baltic States.

The area is not large and it is possible to see in one afternoon. The Republic of Užupis contains lots of unusual sights e.g. the Bernardine Cemetery and the Užupis Angel monument. The entrance to the republic is free of charge. Spend your money at the art and antique shops instead. The republic is located near the Old Town and the best point to enter is at the bridge on Užupio gatvė

Museum of Genocide Victims

Aukų g. 2A
Tel: +370 5 249 74 27
http://www.genocid.lt/muziejus

There is a great variety of museums in Vilnius. They cover different topics and historical events so every guest of Vilnius should find something of interest. One of the most impressive of is the Museum of Genocide Victims. Although this period is a painful part of the history of Lithuania, it is important to be aware of the mistakes made in the past. The exhibitions contain many educational items, but for the majority of the guests the real KGB inner prison seems the most interesting attraction. The entrance fees are very reasonable: an adult ticket costs 6 LTL ($2.30), and a ticket for schoolchildren or students costs 3 LTL ($1.13)

Curonian Spit

The Curonian Spit is 4 km by 98 km long peninsula located in the Baltic Sea. The spit is connected to the land only in the Russian-owned Kaliningrad oblast. You can reach it from the Lithuanian side by taking a ferry from Klaipeda. The return (round-trip) ticket is 2.9 LTL ($1.10), carrying a bicycle is free of charge and the transportation of a car costs 40 LTL ($15).

Curonian Spit (Kursiu Nerija) was formed about 5000 years ago. Climate and different historical events have played an important role in its development. During the 19th century it was clear, that if it was protected it would soon vanish forever. Since 2000 it is has been on the UNESCO World Heritage List.

The Curonian Spit offers magnificent scenery, old fishing settlements, and beaches as well as good tourist facilities. This is a great holiday spot for outdoor lifestyles, especially cyclists with its long bicycle path running parallel to the only highway of the Curonian Spit. There are good bathing spots and white-sand beaches in the western littoral.

Nida Tourist Information Center
Taikos str. 4
Tel.: 8 469 5 23 45
www.visitneringa.com

Neringa is a beautiful area of the Curonian Spit. The well known villages here are Nida and Juodkrantė offering accommodation, shops and cafes. In the summertime various cultural events are organized. The local Tourist Information Center is located in Nida and in the summer season it is open from 10 AM to 6 PM; in other months of the year working hours are a little shorter. In the Tourist Information Centre you will be provided with information about accommodation and events on the Curonian Spit.

Šiauliai

Šiaulai Tourism Information Center
Viliaus Street 213
Šiauliai
Tel: +370 41 523110
tic.siauliai.lt

Šiauliai is a modest, well-established town in the northern part of Lithuania. If translating from Lithuanian Šiauliai means Sun and Šiauliai is often called the Town of Sun. Take a stroll on the streets of Šiauliai and you will see seven buildings and sculptures that are connected with the theme of the Sun.

The town is good for visitors who want to explore the cultural and historical legacy of Lithuania. The main attractions of Šiauliai are the Šiauliai Cathedral of the Apostles St. Peter and St. Paul (a magnificent Renaissance building, built in the 17th century), Sundial Square and various churches, fountains and sculptures. Nearby Cross Hill is a sightseeing highlight as well. The culture life in Šiauliai is active with frequent performances, exhibitions, concerts and festivals.

Šiauliai Aušros Museum

Vytauto Street 89
LT – 77155 Šiauliai
Tel: +370 41 52 69 33
www.ausrosmuziejus.lt

Šiauliai Aušros Museum is the largest museum in the city and it incorporates eight other impressive museums: Ch. Frenkelis Villa, Venclauskiai House, Aušros Avenue Mansion, Photography Museum, Bicycle Museum, Radio and Television Museum, Poet Jovaras' House and Žaliūkių Village Miller's Farmstead.

You can purchase a ticket that covers entry to all six museums of Šiauliai Aušros Museum. An adult ticket costs 15 LTL ($5.70) and you pay 8 LTL ($3) for a childrens ticket. The ticket is valid for 3 days after purchase.

Park of Europe

Joneikiskiu k.
LT- 15148
Tel: +370 5 2377 077
www.europosparkas.lt

Park of Europe (Eiropos Parkas), founded in 1991, is a remarkable and imposing open-air museum of contemporary art. The idea of establishing such museum was to mark the midpoint of Europe in Lithuania.

To reach the Park of Europe from Vilnius, you should approach from the direction of Zalieji Ezerai where a sign points you to the Park of Europe. If you want to get there by bus, you should leave from the Zalgirio bus stop.

The park covers about 55 ha and visitors can relax in the natural surroundings as well as enjoy the art of local and foreign artists. The collection includes more than 90 works.

Chair/Pool (1996) and Drinking Structure with Exposed Kidney Pool (1998) are two giant exhibits by Dennis Oppenheim, a famous conceptualist of contemporary art. He used about 300 meters of rolled steel pipes, 100 square meters of steel mesh and about 2 tons of water in order to create a monstrous chair which has become one of the most popular sculptures of the museum. The second sculpture is also huge, from one side it looks like a house, but from the other side looking as if alive with a "tongue".

Other impressive artwork includes the sculpture LNK Infotree. Nowhere in the world will you find such a huge exhibit made from over 3000 TV sets (weighing 150 tons). It occupies an area of 3,315 sq meters and in the middle features a statue of Lenin to symbolize the ineptitude of communism.

The museum is open every day throughout the year from 10 AM to sunset. Adult ticket costs 25 LTL ($9.5), students have to pay 18 LTL ($6.8) and school children pay 11 LTL ($4.15). Pre-school kids accompanied by a parent or teacher do not pay for entrance. A restaurant, Post Office and shop are available.

Hill of Crosses, Jurgaičiai

The Hill of Crosses is located 12 kilometers to the North from Šiauliai and is one of the most remarkable sacred sites in the Baltic States. Some may find the look of the site quite bizarre. Thousands of crosses of different sizes have been placed next to each other with the numbers growing as all are welcome to add their crosses here.

Some of the crosses are simple and others are huge with carvings and elaborate details resembling ornate artwork. The crosses were brought from various countries by pilgrims who regard the site as sacred. The most famous visitor to the site was Pope John Paul II.

The history of the hill is unclear. In ancient times a wooden castle of Semigallians was located there, but no one knows when the first cross was placed here. The tradition of setting crosses at the roadside is even older.

The resolve of the pilgrims has been admirable. During Soviet times the crosses were repeatedly burnt and removed but locals persevered by replacing the crosses on the hill.

You do not have to be religious to visit this place and leaving a cross is not required. Just stop by to observe this unique tradition and the magnificence of the place.

Buses run infrequently from Šiauliai to the Hill of Crosses so check the bus schedule prior going there.

Franciscan Monastery

Jurgaičiai Village, Meškuičiai Eldership,
Šiauliai District.
Tel.: 8 41 527733

About 300 meters from the Hill of Crosses is a Franciscan Monastery. The idea of building such a monastery came from Pope John Paul II who urged the friars of the Franciscan Sanctuary of La Verna in Italy to establish a monastery at this sacred site. The design and interior of the monastery is rather impressive and therefore it is worth visiting at the same time as the Hill of Crosses. It is open from 8 AM to 9 PM.

Augštaitija National Park

Palūše village
LT- 4759 Ignalina district
Tel: +370 229 53 135
www.anp.lt

Founded in 1974, Auštaitija National Park is the first national park of Lithuania. It is located 100 kilometers east of Vilnius and it occupies the area of more than 4000 hectares, about 70% of it is covered by forest. The place is rich in flora and fauna. The scenery there is unbelievably beautiful and every year it attracts many cyclists and hikers who explore the park independently. It is also possible to book guided tours at the Visitor Information Center or Tourism Center in Palūše, a one hour tour costs about 45 LTL ($17).

The area is perfect for water lovers as the park contains 126 lakes with many of them close by. There are several boat and canoe rental companies in the area of Augštaitija National Park: Evo Baidares, Baidarių Bazė, Ignaturas and Ginto Baidarės are just a few of them. Booking can be arranged either online, by phone, or in person.

Museum of Ancient Beekeeping

Stripeikių kaimas, Ignalina district, LT- 302220
Tel: +370 686 12 105

If you have ever wondered about the history of beekeeping, the Museum of Ancient Beekeeping in Augštaitija National park would be an interesting place to visit. Here the traditional beekeeping methods are explained. There are lots of wooden sculptures showing the history of bees and beekeeping. The admission fee for adults is 3 LTL ($1.13), for students and school children it is 1 LTL ($0.38). Guided tour cost 30 LTL ($11.35). Take notice that museum is open only in the period from May to October.

Panevėžys

Panevėžys Tourism Information Centre
Laisvės a. 11, LT- 35200 Panevėžys
Tel: + 370 45 508080, +370 45 508081
www.panevezysinfo.lt

Panevėžys is located halfway between two capitals - Riga and Vilnius - and is a convenient stopping point for vistiors traveling between Latvia and Lithuania.

Panevėžys is the fifth largest city in Lithuania but is much smaller than Vilnius. In Panevėžys look for the urban landscape and modern establishments as well as the ancient culture and historical legacy. If you want to explore the architecture of Panevėžys start with the churches like St. Peter and St. Paul's Church, the Church of Holy Trinity, Cathedral of Christ the King and others.

Leisure tourists and entertainment seekers will not be disappointed as well. The entertainment possibilities include horse riding in Molainiai, Nausodė or Pas Vaidą; canoe and bicycle rentals; shopping centers such as Babilonas I and Babilonas II and nightclubs including Nightclub Puntukas, Nightclub Tuborg Residence, Nightclub Aragvi.

J. Masiulis Bookstore

On the corner of Elektros and Respublikos gatve

If you are a fan of literature, you will certainly like this book shop. It was founded more than a century ago and is still going strong. The building itself is an interesting architectural example and features books in different languages. In front of the bookstore a Gallery of Photography is located.

Panevėžys Local Lore Museum

Vasario 16-osios g. 23
LT-35185 Panevėžys
Tel: +370 45 46 23 31
http://www.paneveziomuziejus.lt/

Local Lore Museum contains local artifacts including the ethnographical, the historical and the natural. Various media is on display including books, photographs, banknotes, coins, audio and video records, sacral wooden sculptures and many others.

There are three main displays. Cross Making in Samogitia will introduce you to the religious carving traditions which were popular some centuries ago. In the exposition of history you will see different items related to the historical development of Lithuania and in the Exposition of Nature stuffed animals, models and herbariums can be seen. The exposition contains a large collection of butterflies gathered from all around the world. On the first Wednesday of the month the entrance to the museum is free. On other days of the month it costs 4 LTL ($1.5) for adults and 2 LTL ($0.76) for children and students.

Kaunas

Kaunas Tourist Information Center
Laisvės 36
Tel: +370 37 32 34 36
www.kaunastic.lt

Kaunas is a scenic city in the central part of Lithuania. The city attracts visitors and has a notable cultural and historical legacy, as well as widespread leisure and shopping facilities. The cultural life in Kaunas includes many museums, art galleries, theaters and music festivals. Ninth Fort, Old Town, Laisves Aleja (Liberty Boulevard – the main shopping street in the city), Mykolas Zilinskas Art Museum, Vytautas the Great Bridge, Devil's Museum, Christ's Resurrection Church and Sugihara House are just some of the places of interest.

Old Town

Kaunas Old Town consists of old streets and buildings some of which date to medieval times. While sightseeing in the Old Town, marvel at the rich Gothic and Renaissance style architecture. Old Town occupies an area of more than 100 includes the Kaunas Castle, St. Georges Church, The Town Hall, the Thunder House and many other sights. You will find some cozy pubs and souvenir shops here as well.

Kaunas Jazz Festival

www.kaunasjazz.lt

Kaunas Jazz is an annual festival held since 1991 and is the largest jazz festival in Lithuania. The festival attracts famous jazz musicians from all over the world and is a great place to see popular jazz artists live. There are some smaller events organised in autumn and winter, but the main festival takes place in spring when the whole town is alive to the sound of jazz.

Kaunas International Film Festival

www.kinofestivalis.lt

Kaunas International Film Festival is the largest film event in Kaunas and has gained recognition across the Baltic region. The festival presents art-house movies that are regarded as noteworthy by critics with a majority of them being somewhat obscure - do not expect to see typical Hollywood movies here. Each years festival maintains the tradition of showing many Lithuanian and Baltic premieres. In 2013 the Kaunas Film Festival will take place from 28 September to 6 October.

Klaipėda

Klaipėda Tourism and Cultural Information Center
Turgaus Str. 7
LT- 91247 Klaipėda
Tel: +370 46 412186
www.klaipedainfo.lt

Klaipėda is a bustling harbor city in the western part of Lithuania. The city has an old and rich history and was mentioned in ancient documents dating from 1252. The former name of Klaipėda was Nemunėlis. The main attractions in Klaipėda are its old town, wooden buildings and the Sea Festival. Every summer the festival attracts thousands of visitors who enjoy the concerts, markets and other attractions. There are a variety of museums, restaurants, exhibition halls and other entertainment facilities to visit in Klaipėda.

Theatre Square

Theatre Square is located in the center of the old town. The main object of interest there is sculpture called Aennchen von Tharau (Ann from Tharau). The sculpture is also the main element of the fountain constructed in honor of Simon Dach, a local poet. The sculpture was established more than once. The first version was constructed in 1912 but just before World War II it was stolen. In 1989 a recreation of the original was established and it stands in the square today.

Castle Museum

Pilies g. 4
LT- 91240 Klaipėda
Tel: +370 46 410527, +370 46 313323
http://www.mlimuziejus.lt/

Castle Museum is located on the ruins left from the magnificent castle which was built in 1252. In 2002 several parts of the ruins were reconstructed and in one of them a museum was established. The exposition gives insight into the development and history of the castle and the city. You can also see various authentic items from the castle including furniture and jewelry. The museum is open from Tuesday to Saturday from 10 AM to 6 PM. The entrance fee is 6 LTL ($2.3) for adults and 3 LTL ($1.13) for students, schoolchildren, retirees and soldiers on active service. Guided tours in English are available.

Klaipėda Picture Gallery & Sculpture Park

Liepų Street 33
Tel: +370 46 410421
www.ldm.lt

Admirers of art will certainly appreciate Klaipėda Picture Gallery and the Picture Gallery of Pradas Domšaitis Culture Center. Pradas Domšaitis was a remarkable 20th century artist who gained fame not in Lithuania and the wider region.

In the gallery you can see his paintings as well as the work of other Lithuanian artists of his time.

A beautiful sculpture park has been established behind the gallery. The park was constructed in honor of the Lithuanian writer Martynas Mažvydas who was the first author to write a book in Lithuanian. The park occupies the area of 10 ha; different abstract and unusual sculptures are placed there. Adult tickets cost 4 LTL ($1.5) but a children's ticket costs 2 LTL ($0.76).

Open Air Museum of Lithuania

L. Lekavičiaus g. 2
LT-56337 Rumšiškės
Tel: +370 346 47 392, +370 346 47 237
www.llbm.lt

With an area of 195 ha, the Open Air Museum of Lithuania is one of the largest open air museums in Europe. The number of exhibits here is indeed impressive with 183 buildings and more than 86,000 exhibits.

Children and adults will find the museum interesting. The main exhibits include dwelling houses with traditional straw roofs and other household buildings that represent the building traditions from different areas of Lithuania. The museum is set in a delightful scenic location. This is a great way to experience the history of Lithuania. On show are the best examples of local traditions, ancient handicrafts and Lithuanian workmanship.

Many additional services are offered here: souvenir shop, craftsmen workshops, bathhouse, bikes for rent, tavern and tearoom, ethno-cultural book store and secure parking lot.

The entrance fees are different depending on how much you want to see. If you are visiting the museum on foot, the ticket is 10 LTL ($3.8), but if you want to drive in the area by car, you will have to pay an extra 50 LTL. If you are visiting just the park, the ticket will cost 3 LTL ($1.13). Guided tours, as well as educational and thematic programs are available.

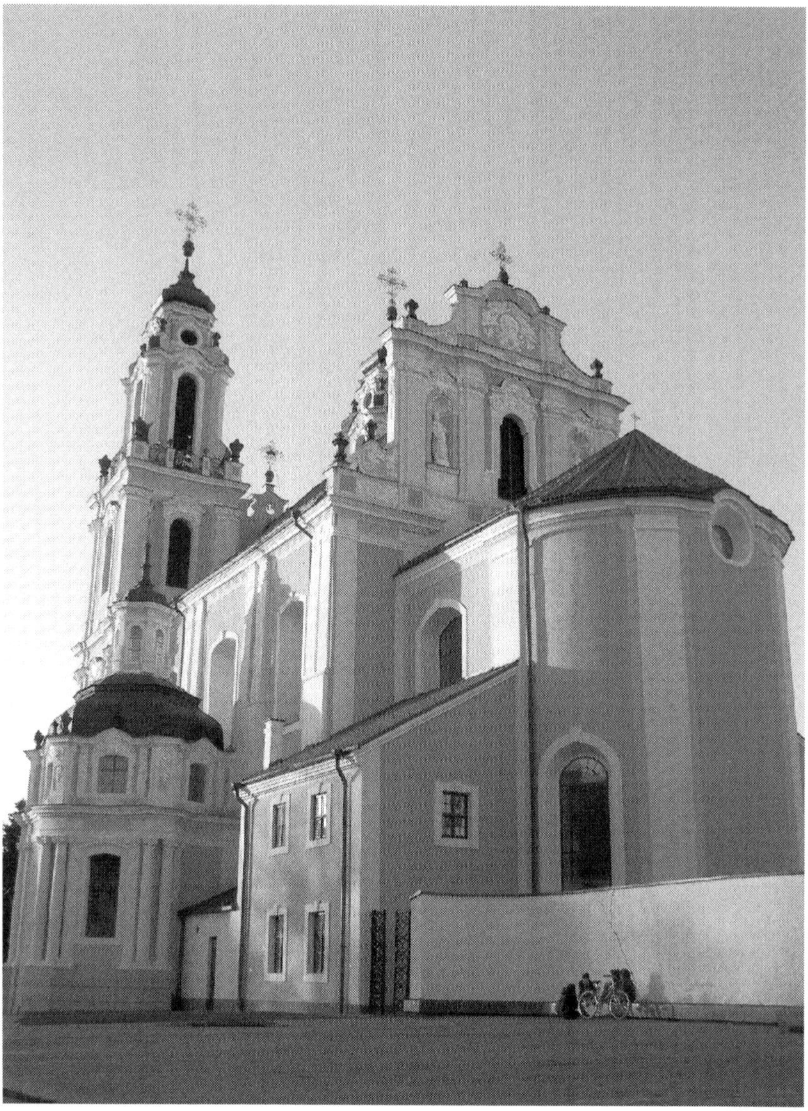

Recommendations For The Budget Traveller

Places to Stay

Dalija Hotel

34 Ateities Street
LT-66314 Druskininkai
Tel: +370 313 51814, +370 612 96558

Dalija is a cozy budget hotel located in the town of Druskininkai. The building is an impressive example of eclectic architecture of the 19th century but the modern approach has been introduced as well in order to create lovely and comfortable hotel for the guests. Double rooms and luxury suites are available, and prices are reasonable. Expect to pay from $22 to $37 per night. The décor is simple but rooms are very comfortable.

Sandra & Co

Šėtos 112
LT- 58116 Kėdainiai
Tel: +370 347 683 48

Sandra & Co is a decent place for budget tourists to pass the night. The interior is simple with the furniture and facilities reminding visitors of harsher Soviet times; however all the rooms are clean and comfortable and have satellite TV. The price for a double room is $26 and a quad-room costs $53.

A5 Hotel

Fabijoniskiu St. 5
Vilnius
Tel: +370 5 2625 241
www.a5hotel.lt

A5 is economy hotel in Vilnius. Although, it is located outside the city center but is within easy reach by public transport. Nearby you will find some entertainment establishments such as cafes, restaurants, several shopping centers (Akropolis, Senukai, OZAS and others) and a sports club.

Despite the reasonable prices all the rooms are very well-equipped and comfortable. You can choose between single (mini), single (double-bed), double, twin rooms and suites. The prices vary from $10 to $18 per night.

Hotel Velga

Geležinio Vilko Str. 3
LT-03131 Vilnius
Tel: +370 5 2311435
www.hotelvelga.lt

Hotel Velga is a two-star budget hotel located near the center of Vilnius. It is a modern establishment with 44 rooms of different categories: single, double, triple and deluxe rooms. The services offered are of a wide range: laundry service/dry cleaning, safety deposit boxes, restaurant, valet parking, Wi-Fi internet and more.

All the rooms are equipped with ensuite shower and toilet, color TV and refrigerator. Expect to pay at least $34 for a single room, $45 for a double room and $56 for a triple room. If you want to stay in a luxury room or suite, the price is about $64.

Hotel Alanta

Alantos g. 33
LT-50175 Kaunas
Tel: +370 37 731142
www.alanta.lt

Located in the city of Kaunas, Hotel Alanta is a good choice since it offers modern, comfortable yet inexpensive accommodation.

The surroundings are quiet but the city center is located just 2 kilometers away and is very easy to reach. Hotel Alanta offers three types of rooms: economy class single for $37, business class double for $45 and business class triple for $61. An extra bed costs $19. There you will be provided with a private bathroom/shower, satellite television, free Wi-Fi, a hairdryer, a telephone and a mini-bar.

Places to Eat

Pinavija Café & Bakery

Vilnius 21
LT- 01402 Vilnius
www.pinavija.lt

Located in the heart of Vilnius, Pinavija Cafe and Bakery has become one of the most popular eating spots in the city. It is a cozy, small, family-run cafe which offers a variety of delicious pastries: cakes, tarts, pies, deserts etc. It is good, cheap place to stop by for a pleasant breakfast while visiting Vilnius. The prices vary from $2 to $12.

Grizzly Grill

Savanoriu 439
Kaunas
+370 690 20000

If you are looking for a substantial but cheap meal in Kaunas, Grizzly Grill is one of the best places to visit. They offer burgers and their barbeque is great. If you love meat and are looking for tasty and big portions, stop to eat at Grizzly Grill. The prices are reasonable and the food is well prepared. Expect to pay from $4 to $10 per meal.

Kybynlar

Karaimu 29
LT- 21001 Trakai
Tel: +370 0 52855179
www.kybynlar.lt

When visiting Lithuania, it is recommended to try some of the local dishes. Café Kybynlar in Trakai will provide you with the finest dishes of the traditional Karaims cuisine. The menu includes a variety of different kybyns (traditional leavened paste cake with different fillings), pies, salads, soups, stews, hot dishes, snacks, side dishes, sauces, sweets and drinks. The interior of Kybynlar is traditional and pleasant. The price for kybyn is about $2, and hot dishes cost about $10.

Cukatos Bakery

Trakų 16
Vilnius
Tel: +370 671 313 91
www.cukatos.lt

Cukatos Bakery is a lovely place in the center of Vilnius. Here you can order different pies, cakes, breads, sweets and desserts. Try the Napoleon or honey cake, the blueberry pie or the rye bread. Indeed, everything served here is really good and the prices will not disappoint.

La Dolce Vita

M. Mažvydo 4/8
Klaipeda
Tel: +370 46 21 21 98

If you are looking for an inexpensive place to eat in Klaipeda, it is worth at visit to La Dolce Vita. It is an elegant restaurant which offers delicious meals at reasonable prices. Despite the fact that the menu is not as Italian as you might expect, the food is tasty and the service is good.

Places to Shop

Shopping facilities in Lithuania are extensive and you can certainly find some good deals while shopping in Lithuania.

Old Market in Klaipeda

Tel: (+370) 46 41 25 07
www.klturgus.lt

If you want a change from the fancy shopping centers with their chic shops and restaurants, you should visit the Old Market in Klaipeda. At the first, this place may seem a bit crowded and dubious but keep in mind that these kinds of authentic markets are simply a legacy of Soviet times and many Lithuanians still find this kind of shopping the best. Here you can buy pretty much everything, from local fruits and vegetables to imported clothes.

Linas-Medis Suvenyrai

Vilniaus 32
Kaunas
Tel: +370 37 20 38 05
www.linasmedis.lt

When looking for some souvenirs to bring home from Lithuania, Linas-Medis shop in Kaunas is a good choice. The variety of souvenirs offered there is great: dolls, traditional items, magnets, craft goods etc. You do not need to spend a lot and the cheapest items cost just $2.

Panorama

Saltoniškių str. 9
LT-08105 Vilnius
Tel: +370 8 5 219 58 11, +370 8 686 39060
www.panorama.lt

Panorama is one of the most popular and fancy shopping centers in Vilnius with broad offerings: accessories, clothes, food products, cosmetics, electronics and more. Here you will find lots of good products for reasonable prices especially in the "sales".

Akropolis

Ozo Street 25,
LT-07150 Vilnius
Tel: +370 5 249 2879
www.akropolis.lt

Akropolis is one of the largest shopping centers in Vilnius. Similar to other shopping centers in Vilnius, it is located in a huge, modern building and includes a large variety of shops. Here you will find lots of clothing stores, food shops, bookstores, cosmetics stores etc.

Senamiesčio Krautuvė

Literatų 5
Vilnius
Tel: +370 5 231 28 36

If you are looking for fresh food and vegetables, this shop, which is situated right in the heart of Vilnius, is a good choice. The proprietors are friendly and will offer good advice. The shop is quite different from the gigantic supermarkets and show what an average Lithuanian will buy in their weekly shop.

Printed in Great Britain
by Amazon